50 Sweet Thai Treat Recipes

By: Kelly Johnson

Table of Contents

- Mango Sticky Rice (Khao Niew Mamuang)
- Thai Coconut Custard (Sangkaya)
- Coconut Jelly (Wun Mamuang)
- Thai Banana in Coconut Milk (Kluai Buat Chi)
- Thai Coconut Ice Cream
- Sweet Sticky Rice with Taro (Khao Niew Mamuang)
- Thai Coconut Pancakes (Khanom Krok)
- Thai Sweet Corn Pudding (Kanom Khao Pod)
- Thai Red Bean Dessert (Bua Loy)
- Thai Sweet Rice Cake (Kanom Khao Neaw)
- Thai Fried Bananas (Kluai Tod)
- Coconut Rice Balls (Bua Loy Nam Kathi)
- Thai Steamed Banana Cake (Kanom Kluai)
- Thai Mango Pudding
- Sweet Sticky Rice with Durian (Khao Niew Durian)
- Thai Sesame Balls (Bua Loy)
- Thai Custard Bread (Kanom Khao Neaw)
- Thai Chocolate Banana Cake
- Thai Sweet Potato Balls (Kanom Khao Niew)
- Thai Tea Cake
- Thai Pumpkin Custard (Sangkaya Fak Thong)
- Thai Coconut Rice (Khao Mamuang)
- Thai Chewy Rice Cake (Kanom Niew)
- Thai Rice Flour Cake (Kanom Jeen)
- Thai Creamy Corn Cake
- Thai Sweet Coconut Rolls (Khanom Pang Sangkhaya)
- Thai Tapioca Pudding (Sangkhaya)
- Thai Sweet Coconut Waffles (Khanom Waffles)
- Thai Banana Coconut Pancakes
- Thai Fluffy Cake (Khanom Khrok)
- Thai Fruit Salad with Coconut Cream
- Thai Steamed Coconut Cake (Kanom Kati)
- Thai Coconut Pudding with Taro (Kanom Taro)
- Thai Pineapple Cake
- Thai Green Tea Cake

- Thai Coconut Mousse
- Thai Coconut Tapioca Pudding
- Thai Grilled Sticky Rice (Khao Jee)
- Thai Sweet Coconut and Taro Dessert
- Thai Sweet Coconut Cream with Jackfruit (Khanom Jek)
- Thai Almond Tofu Dessert
- Thai Coconut and Sesame Balls (Bua Loy)
- Thai Chocolate Coconut Cake
- Thai Coconut Rice Cakes with Sugar (Kanom Jeen)
- Thai Honey and Coconut Cake
- Thai Chia Seed Pudding
- Thai Sweet Black Sesame Soup
- Thai Coconut and Sweet Potato Dessert
- Thai Watermelon Coconut Dessert
- Thai Pandan Cake

Mango Sticky Rice (Khao Niew Mamuang)

Ingredients

- 1 cup glutinous (sticky) rice (soaked for at least 4 hours)
- 2 ripe mangoes (sliced)
- 1 cup coconut milk
- 1/2 cup sugar
- 1/4 tsp salt
- Sesame seeds or mung beans (for garnish, optional)

Instructions

1. Steam the soaked sticky rice for about 20-30 minutes until cooked and translucent.
2. In a saucepan, heat coconut milk, sugar, and salt over low heat until the sugar dissolves. Reserve some coconut milk for drizzling later.
3. Combine the warm sticky rice with the coconut milk mixture, stirring gently. Let it sit for about 30 minutes to absorb the flavors.
4. Serve the sticky rice with sliced mangoes on the side, drizzled with reserved coconut milk and garnished with sesame seeds or mung beans.

Thai Coconut Custard (Sangkaya)

Ingredients

- 1 cup coconut milk
- 1/2 cup sugar
- 1/4 tsp salt
- 3 large eggs
- 1/2 cup rice flour (optional for thickness)

Instructions

1. Preheat the steamer. In a bowl, whisk together coconut milk, sugar, salt, and eggs until smooth.
2. If using, add rice flour and mix until well combined.
3. Pour the mixture into small cups or a greased baking dish.
4. Steam for about 20-30 minutes until set. Serve warm or chilled.

Coconut Jelly (Wun Mamuang)

Ingredients

- 1 cup coconut milk
- 1 cup water
- 1/2 cup sugar
- 1-2 tsp agar-agar powder (or gelatin)
- 1/4 tsp salt

Instructions

1. In a saucepan, mix water, sugar, and agar-agar. Bring to a boil while stirring until dissolved.
2. Add coconut milk and salt, mixing well.
3. Pour the mixture into molds and let it cool until set in the refrigerator.
4. Cut into squares and serve chilled.

Thai Banana in Coconut Milk (Kluai Buat Chi)

Ingredients

- 4-5 ripe bananas (peeled and sliced)
- 2 cups coconut milk
- 1/2 cup sugar
- 1/4 tsp salt
- 1-2 pandan leaves (optional, for flavor)

Instructions

1. In a saucepan, combine coconut milk, sugar, salt, and pandan leaves. Heat gently until the sugar dissolves.
2. Add sliced bananas and simmer for about 5-10 minutes until the bananas are tender.
3. Serve warm or chilled.

Thai Coconut Ice Cream

Ingredients

- 2 cups coconut milk
- 1/2 cup sugar
- 1/2 cup heavy cream
- 1 tsp vanilla extract
- Pinch of salt

Instructions

1. In a bowl, mix coconut milk, sugar, heavy cream, vanilla extract, and salt until well combined.
2. Pour the mixture into an ice cream maker and churn according to the manufacturer's instructions until it reaches a soft-serve consistency.
3. Transfer to a container and freeze for at least 4-6 hours until firm. Serve with toppings like peanuts or coconut flakes.

Sweet Sticky Rice with Taro (Khao Niew Mamuang)

Ingredients

- 1 cup glutinous rice (soaked for at least 4 hours)
- 1 cup coconut milk
- 1/2 cup sugar
- 1/4 tsp salt
- 1 cup taro (peeled and cubed)

Instructions

1. Steam the soaked sticky rice for about 20-30 minutes until cooked.
2. In a saucepan, combine coconut milk, sugar, and salt, heating until the sugar dissolves.
3. Add cubed taro to the steamer for the last 10-15 minutes until tender.
4. Mix the warm sticky rice with the coconut milk mixture. Serve with taro on the side.

Thai Coconut Pancakes (Khanom Krok)

Ingredients

- 1 cup rice flour
- 1 cup coconut milk
- 1/2 cup sugar
- 1/2 tsp salt
- Optional toppings: green onions, corn, or taro

Instructions

1. In a bowl, mix rice flour, coconut milk, sugar, and salt until smooth.
2. Heat a mini pancake pan or muffin tin over medium heat. Pour a spoonful of batter into each cup.
3. Cook until the edges are set, then add optional toppings and cover with more batter.
4. Cook until golden and serve warm.

Thai Sweet Corn Pudding (Kanom Khao Pod)

Ingredients

- 1 cup corn kernels (fresh or canned)
- 1 cup coconut milk
- 1/2 cup rice flour
- 1/2 cup sugar
- 1/4 tsp salt

Instructions

1. Preheat the steamer. In a bowl, mix corn, coconut milk, rice flour, sugar, and salt until smooth.
2. Pour the mixture into small cups and steam for about 20-25 minutes until set.
3. Allow to cool slightly before serving.

Thai Red Bean Dessert (Bua Loy)

Ingredients

- 1 cup glutinous rice flour
- 1/2 cup water
- 1 cup coconut milk
- 1/2 cup sugar
- 1/4 tsp salt
- 1/2 cup red beans (cooked)

Instructions

1. In a bowl, mix glutinous rice flour and water to form a dough. Roll into small balls.
2. Boil water in a pot, add the balls, and cook until they float.
3. In another pot, heat coconut milk, sugar, and salt until the sugar dissolves.
4. Add the cooked balls and red beans to the coconut milk mixture. Serve warm.

Thai Sweet Rice Cake (Kanom Khao Neaw)

Ingredients

- 1 cup glutinous (sticky) rice (soaked for at least 4 hours)
- 1 cup coconut milk
- 1/2 cup sugar
- 1/4 tsp salt
- 1/2 tsp baking powder (optional)

Instructions

1. Steam the soaked sticky rice for about 30 minutes until cooked and translucent.
2. In a bowl, mix coconut milk, sugar, salt, and baking powder until well combined.
3. Pour the mixture over the cooked sticky rice and stir gently to combine.
4. Steam the combined mixture for another 20-30 minutes until set. Allow to cool before slicing and serving.

Thai Fried Bananas (Kluai Tod)

Ingredients

- 4-5 ripe bananas (preferably Thai bananas)
- 1 cup rice flour
- 1/4 cup sugar
- 1/4 tsp salt
- Water (as needed)
- Oil for frying

Instructions

1. In a bowl, mix rice flour, sugar, and salt. Gradually add water until you achieve a thick batter.
2. Peel and cut the bananas in half lengthwise.
3. Heat oil in a pan over medium heat. Dip the banana pieces in the batter, then fry until golden brown and crispy.
4. Drain on paper towels and serve warm.

Coconut Rice Balls (Bua Loy Nam Kathi)

Ingredients

- 1 cup glutinous rice flour
- 1/2 cup water
- 1 cup coconut milk
- 1/2 cup sugar
- 1/4 tsp salt
- Food coloring (optional)

Instructions

1. In a bowl, mix glutinous rice flour and water to form a smooth dough. If desired, divide the dough and add food coloring.
2. Roll the dough into small balls.
3. Boil water in a pot, add the rice balls, and cook until they float. Remove and set aside.
4. In another pot, heat coconut milk, sugar, and salt until the sugar dissolves.
5. Add the cooked rice balls to the coconut milk and serve warm.

Thai Steamed Banana Cake (Kanom Kluai)

Ingredients

- 2 cups ripe bananas (mashed)
- 1 cup rice flour
- 1 cup coconut milk
- 1/2 cup sugar
- 1/4 tsp salt
- 1 tsp baking powder (optional)

Instructions

1. In a bowl, combine mashed bananas, rice flour, coconut milk, sugar, salt, and baking powder until well mixed.
2. Pour the batter into small cups or a greased baking dish.
3. Steam for about 20-25 minutes until set. Allow to cool before serving.

Thai Mango Pudding

Ingredients

- 2 ripe mangoes (pureed)
- 1 cup coconut milk
- 1/2 cup sugar
- 1/4 cup water
- 2 tsp agar-agar powder (or gelatin)

Instructions

1. In a saucepan, combine water, sugar, and agar-agar. Bring to a boil while stirring until dissolved.
2. Remove from heat and mix in the mango puree and coconut milk until well combined.
3. Pour into molds and let cool until set in the refrigerator. Serve chilled.

Sweet Sticky Rice with Durian (Khao Niew Durian)

Ingredients

- 1 cup glutinous rice (soaked for at least 4 hours)
- 1 cup coconut milk
- 1/2 cup sugar
- 1/4 tsp salt
- 1 cup durian (fresh or frozen)

Instructions

1. Steam the soaked sticky rice for about 20-30 minutes until cooked and translucent.
2. In a saucepan, heat coconut milk, sugar, and salt until the sugar dissolves. Reserve some coconut milk for drizzling later.
3. Combine the warm sticky rice with the coconut milk mixture and let it sit for about 30 minutes.
4. Serve the sticky rice with pieces of durian on the side, drizzled with reserved coconut milk.

Thai Sesame Balls (Bua Loy)

Ingredients

- 1 cup glutinous rice flour
- 1/2 cup water
- Sesame seeds (for coating)
- Oil for frying

Instructions

1. In a bowl, mix glutinous rice flour and water to form a smooth dough.
2. Roll the dough into small balls and coat with sesame seeds.
3. Heat oil in a pan over medium heat and fry the balls until golden brown.
4. Drain on paper towels and serve warm.

Thai Custard Bread (Kanom Khao Neaw)

Ingredients

- 2 cups all-purpose flour
- 1 cup coconut milk
- 1/2 cup sugar
- 1/4 tsp salt
- 1/2 cup warm water
- 1 tsp yeast (optional)

Instructions

1. In a bowl, mix all-purpose flour, coconut milk, sugar, and salt. Knead to form a dough.
2. If using, dissolve yeast in warm water and add to the dough. Knead until smooth.
3. Let the dough rise for about 1 hour, then shape into small buns.
4. Steam for about 20-25 minutes until cooked through. Serve warm.

Thai Chocolate Banana Cake

Ingredients

- 2 ripe bananas (mashed)
- 1/2 cup cocoa powder
- 1 cup all-purpose flour
- 1/2 cup sugar
- 1/2 cup coconut milk
- 1/4 cup vegetable oil
- 1 tsp baking powder
- 1/4 tsp salt

Instructions

1. Preheat the oven to 350°F (175°C). Grease a cake pan.
2. In a bowl, mix mashed bananas, cocoa powder, flour, sugar, coconut milk, oil, baking powder, and salt until well combined.
3. Pour the batter into the prepared pan and bake for about 25-30 minutes or until a toothpick comes out clean.
4. Allow to cool before slicing and serving.

Thai Sweet Potato Balls (Kanom Khao Niew)

Ingredients

- 1 cup sweet potato (mashed)
- 1 cup glutinous rice flour
- 1/4 cup sugar
- 1/2 cup coconut milk
- Pinch of salt
- Oil for frying

Instructions

1. In a bowl, mix the mashed sweet potato, glutinous rice flour, sugar, coconut milk, and salt until well combined to form a dough.
2. Roll the dough into small balls.
3. Heat oil in a pan over medium heat and fry the balls until golden brown.
4. Drain on paper towels and serve warm.

Thai Tea Cake

Ingredients

- 1 cup all-purpose flour
- 1/2 cup sugar
- 1/2 cup unsalted butter (softened)
- 1/4 cup strong brewed Thai tea (cooled)
- 2 large eggs
- 1 tsp baking powder
- 1/4 tsp salt

Instructions

1. Preheat the oven to 350°F (175°C). Grease and flour a cake pan.
2. In a bowl, cream together the softened butter and sugar until light and fluffy.
3. Beat in the eggs one at a time, then stir in the brewed tea.
4. In another bowl, mix flour, baking powder, and salt. Gradually add to the wet mixture until well combined.
5. Pour the batter into the prepared pan and bake for 25-30 minutes or until a toothpick comes out clean. Allow to cool before serving.

Thai Pumpkin Custard (Sangkaya Fak Thong)

Ingredients

- 2 cups pumpkin (peeled and cubed)
- 1 cup coconut milk
- 1/2 cup sugar
- 1/4 tsp salt
- 2 eggs
- 1/2 tsp vanilla extract

Instructions

1. Steam the pumpkin cubes until soft, then mash until smooth.
2. In a bowl, mix the mashed pumpkin, coconut milk, sugar, salt, eggs, and vanilla extract until well combined.
3. Pour the mixture into a pumpkin shell or custard cups.
4. Steam for about 30-40 minutes until set. Allow to cool before slicing and serving.

Thai Coconut Rice (Khao Mamuang)

Ingredients

- 2 cups glutinous rice (soaked for at least 4 hours)
- 1 cup coconut milk
- 1/2 cup sugar
- 1/4 tsp salt

Instructions

1. Steam the soaked sticky rice for about 30 minutes until cooked and translucent.
2. In a saucepan, heat coconut milk, sugar, and salt until the sugar dissolves.
3. Pour the coconut milk mixture over the warm sticky rice and let it sit for about 30 minutes.
4. Serve warm or chilled, optionally with fresh mango slices.

Thai Chewy Rice Cake (Kanom Niew)

Ingredients

- 1 cup glutinous rice flour
- 1/2 cup sugar
- 1 cup coconut milk
- 1/4 tsp salt

Instructions

1. In a bowl, mix glutinous rice flour, sugar, coconut milk, and salt until smooth.
2. Pour the mixture into a greased steaming tray or dish.
3. Steam for about 20-25 minutes until set. Allow to cool before slicing and serving.

Thai Rice Flour Cake (Kanom Jeen)

Ingredients

- 1 cup rice flour
- 1/2 cup sugar
- 1 cup coconut milk
- 1/4 tsp salt
- 1 tsp baking powder

Instructions

1. In a bowl, mix rice flour, sugar, coconut milk, salt, and baking powder until well combined.
2. Pour the batter into greased molds or a tray.
3. Steam for about 20-25 minutes until set. Allow to cool before slicing and serving.

Thai Creamy Corn Cake

Ingredients

- 1 cup corn (fresh or canned)
- 1 cup coconut milk
- 1/2 cup rice flour
- 1/4 cup sugar
- 1/4 tsp salt
- 1 tsp baking powder

Instructions

1. In a bowl, combine corn, coconut milk, rice flour, sugar, salt, and baking powder until well mixed.
2. Pour the mixture into greased cups or a tray.
3. Steam for about 20-25 minutes until set. Allow to cool before serving.

Thai Sweet Coconut Rolls (Khanom Pang Sangkhaya)

Ingredients

- 2 cups all-purpose flour
- 1 cup coconut milk
- 1/2 cup sugar
- 1/4 tsp salt
- 1/2 tsp baking powder
- Banana leaves (for wrapping)

Instructions

1. In a bowl, mix all-purpose flour, coconut milk, sugar, salt, and baking powder until smooth.
2. Pour a small amount of batter onto a banana leaf, roll it up, and secure it with a toothpick.
3. Steam for about 20-25 minutes until set. Allow to cool before serving.

Thai Tapioca Pudding (Sangkhaya)

Ingredients

- 1 cup tapioca pearls
- 2 cups coconut milk
- 1 cup sugar
- 1/4 tsp salt
- 2 cups water
- Pandan leaves (optional, for flavor)

Instructions

1. Rinse the tapioca pearls under cold water until the water runs clear.
2. In a pot, combine water and tapioca pearls. Cook over medium heat, stirring occasionally, until the tapioca turns translucent (about 15-20 minutes).
3. In another saucepan, heat coconut milk, sugar, salt, and pandan leaves (if using) until the sugar dissolves.
4. Once the tapioca is cooked, drain and add it to the coconut milk mixture. Stir well and cook for an additional 5 minutes.
5. Serve warm or chilled, optionally topped with more coconut cream.

Thai Sweet Coconut Waffles (Khanom Waffles)

Ingredients

- 1 cup all-purpose flour
- 1 cup coconut milk
- 1/2 cup sugar
- 1/4 tsp salt
- 1 tsp baking powder
- 1/2 tsp vanilla extract

Instructions

1. In a bowl, mix together flour, sugar, salt, and baking powder.
2. In another bowl, combine coconut milk and vanilla extract. Gradually add the wet mixture to the dry ingredients until well blended.
3. Preheat a waffle iron and lightly grease it.
4. Pour a ladle of batter onto the waffle iron and cook until golden brown. Repeat with remaining batter.
5. Serve warm with additional coconut cream or toppings of choice.

Thai Banana Coconut Pancakes

Ingredients

- 1 cup all-purpose flour
- 1 cup coconut milk
- 1 ripe banana (mashed)
- 1/4 cup sugar
- 1 tsp baking powder
- 1/4 tsp salt
- Oil for frying

Instructions

1. In a bowl, combine flour, sugar, baking powder, and salt.
2. In another bowl, mix coconut milk and mashed banana until smooth.
3. Pour the wet mixture into the dry ingredients and stir until just combined.
4. Heat a little oil in a skillet over medium heat. Pour in a ladle of batter and cook until bubbles form on the surface, then flip and cook until golden brown.
5. Serve warm with honey, maple syrup, or additional coconut cream.

Thai Fluffy Cake (Khanom Khrok)

Ingredients

- 1 cup rice flour
- 1/2 cup sugar
- 1 cup coconut milk
- 1/4 tsp salt
- 1 tsp baking powder
- 1/2 cup grated coconut (optional, for topping)

Instructions

1. In a bowl, mix rice flour, sugar, salt, and baking powder.
2. Gradually add coconut milk to the dry mixture, stirring until smooth.
3. Preheat a khrok pan (or small round pancake pan) and lightly grease it.
4. Pour the batter into each mold and cover with a lid. Cook for about 5-7 minutes until the cakes are fluffy and cooked through.
5. Serve warm, optionally topped with grated coconut.

Thai Fruit Salad with Coconut Cream

Ingredients

- 2 cups mixed fruits (e.g., mango, pineapple, banana, and watermelon)
- 1 cup coconut milk
- 1/4 cup sugar
- 1/4 tsp salt
- 1 tsp vanilla extract
- 1 tbsp lime juice

Instructions

1. In a bowl, mix coconut milk, sugar, salt, vanilla extract, and lime juice until well combined.
2. In another bowl, combine the mixed fruits.
3. Drizzle the coconut cream over the fruits and toss gently to combine.
4. Serve chilled.

Thai Steamed Coconut Cake (Kanom Kati)

Ingredients

- 1 cup rice flour
- 1 cup coconut milk
- 1/2 cup sugar
- 1/4 tsp salt
- 1 tsp baking powder

Instructions

1. In a bowl, mix rice flour, sugar, salt, and baking powder.
2. Gradually add coconut milk to the dry ingredients and stir until smooth.
3. Pour the batter into greased small cups or molds.
4. Steam for about 20-25 minutes until set. Allow to cool before serving.

Thai Coconut Pudding with Taro (Kanom Taro)

Ingredients

- 1 cup taro (peeled and diced)
- 1 cup coconut milk
- 1/2 cup sugar
- 1 cup rice flour
- 1/4 tsp salt
- 1 tsp baking powder

Instructions

1. Steam the diced taro until soft, then mash it.
2. In a bowl, mix mashed taro, coconut milk, sugar, rice flour, salt, and baking powder until smooth.
3. Pour the mixture into greased cups or molds.
4. Steam for about 20-25 minutes until set. Allow to cool before serving.

Thai Pineapple Cake

Ingredients

- 1 cup all-purpose flour
- 1/2 cup sugar
- 1/2 cup butter (softened)
- 1 cup crushed pineapple (drained)
- 2 large eggs
- 1 tsp baking powder
- 1/4 tsp salt
- 1 tsp vanilla extract

Instructions

1. Preheat the oven to 350°F (175°C). Grease and flour a cake pan.
2. In a bowl, cream together butter and sugar until light and fluffy. Beat in the eggs one at a time, then stir in the vanilla and crushed pineapple.
3. In another bowl, mix flour, baking powder, and salt. Gradually add to the wet mixture until well combined.
4. Pour the batter into the prepared pan and bake for 25-30 minutes or until a toothpick comes out clean. Allow to cool before serving.

Thai Green Tea Cake

Ingredients

- 1 cup all-purpose flour
- 1/2 cup sugar
- 1/2 cup butter (softened)
- 2 large eggs
- 1/4 cup milk
- 2 tbsp green tea powder (matcha)
- 1 tsp baking powder
- 1/4 tsp salt
- Powdered sugar (for dusting, optional)

Instructions

1. Preheat the oven to 350°F (175°C). Grease and flour a cake pan.
2. In a bowl, cream together butter and sugar until light and fluffy. Beat in the eggs one at a time.
3. Mix green tea powder with milk and add it to the batter.
4. In another bowl, whisk together flour, baking powder, and salt. Gradually add the dry ingredients to the wet mixture until combined.
5. Pour the batter into the prepared pan and bake for 25-30 minutes or until a toothpick comes out clean. Allow to cool and dust with powdered sugar before serving.

Thai Coconut Mousse

Ingredients

- 1 cup coconut milk
- 1/2 cup heavy cream
- 1/4 cup sugar
- 1 tsp gelatin (dissolved in 2 tbsp water)
- 1 tsp vanilla extract
- Toasted coconut flakes (for topping)

Instructions

1. In a saucepan, heat coconut milk and sugar until dissolved. Remove from heat and stir in dissolved gelatin and vanilla extract.
2. Let the mixture cool slightly.
3. In a separate bowl, whip the heavy cream until soft peaks form. Gently fold the whipped cream into the coconut mixture until combined.
4. Pour into serving cups and refrigerate for at least 2 hours until set. Top with toasted coconut flakes before serving.

Thai Coconut Tapioca Pudding

Ingredients

- 1 cup tapioca pearls
- 2 cups coconut milk
- 1/4 cup sugar
- 1/4 tsp salt
- 2 cups water
- Fresh mango or fruit for topping (optional)

Instructions

1. Rinse tapioca pearls under cold water until the water runs clear.
2. In a pot, combine water and tapioca pearls, and cook over medium heat, stirring occasionally until the pearls become translucent (about 15-20 minutes).
3. In another saucepan, heat coconut milk, sugar, and salt until dissolved.
4. Once the tapioca is cooked, drain and add to the coconut milk mixture. Stir well and cook for an additional 5 minutes.
5. Serve warm or chilled, topped with fresh mango or your favorite fruit.

Thai Grilled Sticky Rice (Khao Jee)

Ingredients

- 2 cups sticky rice (glutinous rice)
- 1 cup coconut milk
- 1/4 cup sugar
- 1/4 tsp salt
- Banana leaves or aluminum foil (for wrapping)

Instructions

1. Soak sticky rice in water for at least 4 hours or overnight. Drain and steam for about 30 minutes until cooked.
2. In a bowl, mix cooked sticky rice with coconut milk, sugar, and salt until well combined.
3. Form the mixture into small patties and wrap each in banana leaves or aluminum foil.
4. Grill over medium heat for about 5-7 minutes on each side until heated through and slightly charred.
5. Serve warm.

Thai Sweet Coconut and Taro Dessert

Ingredients

- 1 cup taro (peeled and diced)
- 1 cup coconut milk
- 1/2 cup sugar
- 1/2 cup rice flour
- 1/4 tsp salt
- 1 tsp baking powder

Instructions

1. Steam the diced taro until soft, then mash it.
2. In a bowl, combine mashed taro, coconut milk, sugar, rice flour, salt, and baking powder until smooth.
3. Pour the mixture into greased small cups or molds.
4. Steam for about 20-25 minutes until set. Allow to cool before serving.

Thai Sweet Coconut Cream with Jackfruit (Khanom Jek)

Ingredients

- 1 cup jackfruit (fresh or canned, diced)
- 1 cup coconut milk
- 1/2 cup sugar
- 1/4 cup rice flour
- 1/4 tsp salt
- 1 tsp gelatin (dissolved in 2 tbsp water)

Instructions

1. In a saucepan, heat coconut milk and sugar until dissolved. Remove from heat and stir in dissolved gelatin and salt.
2. Add rice flour to the mixture and whisk until smooth.
3. Add diced jackfruit and stir gently.
4. Pour the mixture into a greased dish and refrigerate until set.
5. Cut into squares or serve as is.

Thai Almond Tofu Dessert

Ingredients

- 1 cup almond milk
- 1/4 cup sugar
- 1 tsp gelatin (dissolved in 2 tbsp water)
- 1/2 tsp almond extract
- Sliced almonds (for garnish)

Instructions

1. In a saucepan, heat almond milk and sugar until dissolved. Remove from heat and stir in dissolved gelatin and almond extract.
2. Pour the mixture into a mold or dish and refrigerate until set.
3. Once set, cut into cubes and garnish with sliced almonds before serving.

Thai Coconut and Sesame Balls (Bua Loy)

Ingredients

- 1 cup glutinous rice flour
- 1/4 cup sugar
- 1/4 cup coconut milk
- 1/4 cup water (more if needed)
- Sesame seeds (for coating)

Instructions

1. In a bowl, mix glutinous rice flour, sugar, coconut milk, and enough water to form a soft dough.
2. Pinch off small pieces of dough and roll them into balls.
3. Roll the balls in sesame seeds to coat them.
4. Steam the balls for about 10-15 minutes until cooked through.
5. Serve warm, drizzled with additional coconut milk if desired.

Thai Chocolate Coconut Cake

Ingredients

- 1 cup all-purpose flour
- 1/2 cup cocoa powder
- 1 cup sugar
- 1/2 cup butter (softened)
- 2 large eggs
- 1 cup coconut milk
- 1 tsp baking powder
- 1/2 tsp baking soda
- 1/4 tsp salt
- Shredded coconut (for topping)

Instructions

1. Preheat the oven to 350°F (175°C) and grease a cake pan.
2. In a bowl, cream together butter and sugar until light and fluffy. Beat in the eggs one at a time.
3. Mix cocoa powder and coconut milk, then add to the butter mixture.
4. In another bowl, combine flour, baking powder, baking soda, and salt. Gradually mix the dry ingredients into the wet ingredients until well combined.
5. Pour the batter into the prepared pan and bake for 25-30 minutes, or until a toothpick comes out clean. Let cool and top with shredded coconut before serving.

Thai Coconut Rice Cakes with Sugar (Kanom Jeen)

Ingredients

- 1 cup rice flour
- 1 cup coconut milk
- 1/4 cup sugar
- 1/4 tsp salt
- Banana leaves or small cups (for steaming)

Instructions

1. In a bowl, combine rice flour, coconut milk, sugar, and salt until smooth.
2. Pour the mixture into small cups or place onto banana leaves.
3. Steam for about 20-25 minutes or until set.
4. Allow to cool and serve warm or at room temperature, optionally drizzled with more coconut milk.

Thai Honey and Coconut Cake

Ingredients

- 1 cup all-purpose flour
- 1/2 cup honey
- 1/2 cup coconut milk
- 1/4 cup sugar
- 1/2 cup butter (softened)
- 2 large eggs
- 1 tsp baking powder
- 1/4 tsp salt
- Shredded coconut (for topping)

Instructions

1. Preheat the oven to 350°F (175°C) and grease a cake pan.
2. In a bowl, cream together butter and sugar. Add honey and mix well.
3. Beat in the eggs one at a time. Then, add coconut milk and mix until combined.
4. In another bowl, combine flour, baking powder, and salt. Gradually mix the dry ingredients into the wet ingredients until well combined.
5. Pour the batter into the prepared pan and bake for 25-30 minutes. Let cool, and top with shredded coconut before serving.

Thai Chia Seed Pudding

Ingredients

- 1/2 cup chia seeds
- 2 cups coconut milk
- 1/4 cup honey or maple syrup
- 1 tsp vanilla extract
- Fresh fruits (for topping)

Instructions

1. In a bowl, combine chia seeds, coconut milk, honey, and vanilla extract. Stir well to combine.
2. Let the mixture sit for about 10 minutes, then stir again to prevent clumping.
3. Cover and refrigerate for at least 2 hours or overnight until it thickens.
4. Serve chilled, topped with fresh fruits.

Thai Sweet Black Sesame Soup

Ingredients

- 1/2 cup black sesame seeds
- 4 cups water
- 1/2 cup sugar
- 1 cup coconut milk

Instructions

1. In a pan, toast black sesame seeds until fragrant. Grind them to a fine powder using a mortar and pestle or blender.
2. In a pot, combine ground sesame, water, and sugar. Simmer over medium heat for about 30 minutes.
3. Stir in coconut milk and cook for an additional 5-10 minutes. Adjust sweetness if desired.
4. Serve warm or chilled.

Thai Coconut and Sweet Potato Dessert

Ingredients

- 1 cup sweet potato (peeled and cubed)
- 1 cup coconut milk
- 1/4 cup sugar
- 1/4 cup rice flour
- 1/4 tsp salt

Instructions

1. Steam sweet potato cubes until tender, then mash them.
2. In a bowl, combine mashed sweet potato, coconut milk, sugar, rice flour, and salt until smooth.
3. Pour the mixture into a greased dish and steam for about 30 minutes or until set.
4. Allow to cool before serving.

Thai Watermelon Coconut Dessert

Ingredients

- 2 cups watermelon (cubed)
- 1 cup coconut milk
- 1/4 cup sugar
- 1/4 cup tapioca pearls (cooked)
- Mint leaves (for garnish)

Instructions

1. In a blender, puree watermelon until smooth. Strain to remove any pulp.
2. In a bowl, mix watermelon juice, coconut milk, and sugar until dissolved.
3. Add cooked tapioca pearls to the mixture and stir gently.
4. Serve chilled, garnished with mint leaves.

Thai Pandan Cake

Ingredients

- 1 cup all-purpose flour
- 1 cup sugar
- 1/2 cup coconut milk
- 1/2 cup pandan juice (blended pandan leaves with water)
- 1/2 cup butter (melted)
- 3 large eggs
- 1 tsp baking powder
- 1/4 tsp salt

Instructions

1. Preheat the oven to 350°F (175°C) and grease a cake pan.
2. In a bowl, beat eggs and sugar until light and fluffy. Gradually add melted butter and mix well.
3. Add coconut milk and pandan juice, stirring to combine.
4. In another bowl, combine flour, baking powder, and salt. Gradually mix dry ingredients into the wet mixture until well combined.
5. Pour the batter into the prepared pan and bake for 25-30 minutes. Let cool before serving.

www.ingramcontent.com/pod-product-compliance
Lightning Source LLC
LaVergne TN
LVHW081504060526
838201LV00056BA/2932